NLP

The Skill Of Interpreting Other People And Learn The Neurological Programming And Personality Traits That Can Help You Understand And Control Other People's Thoughts

GertProhaska

TABLE OF CONTENT

How Different Types Of NLP Training Are Categorised 1

Eye Movements Used In NLP For Reading The Other Person.. 12

Is It Possible That Someone Could Use Our Reality Map Against Us? 21

The First Method Is Called Anchoring. 24

What Exactly Is The Milton Model When It Comes To NLP And Hypnosis? 39

Visual Methods And Strategies 46

Advice To Help Improve One's Communication Skills 57

Having A Blank Canvas In Front Of You 61

Manipulation Of Emotional States 74

Manipulation In The Course Of Our Everyday Lives 82

Historically Notable Instances Of Deceit 98

Methods For Influencing The Mind 105

NLP And Education 129

"What Was It About The Other Presenters That Didn't Impress You?" 144

How Different Types Of NLP Training Are Categorised

After appreciating the value of NLP training, the next important step is to get an understanding of the activities required for achievement. There are a great number of organisations that have earned a reputation for their capacity to plan, manage, and deliver these kinds of programmes. When pursuing the course, it is to one's advantage to enrol in only one educational establishment. The following is a rundown of the three stages of NLP training:

NLP Practitioner (Practitioner)

There are no prerequisites in terms of prior experience to sign up for this course, which is considered to be the foundational level of NLP education. Studying the principles of NLP, as well as the methodologies and components that are utilised, is a necessary step in this process. They are debating the best way to put all of their sophistication and talent to use. In order for them to effectively carry out their tasks, they take into account all of the relevant skills and methodologies, while at the same time ensuring that their lives are touched in a positive way.

The themes that will be covered in this course include how to handle problems in relationships, families, and businesses. When one is well-versed in all of the strategies, it is also much simpler to experience positive personal advancement in one's academic endeavours. This training will cover both the theory and the practical application of NLP techniques. It helps people overcome their fears and eliminates feelings of dread and anxiety in the process.

Master of the NLP

During this second phase, the amount of material that must be learned expands, along with the scope of the data and the complexity of the models that must be utilised. It is more complex and makes use of a wider range of words and models. They ultimately achieve capabilities that cause a shift in both their perspective on life and their internalised values and beliefs. the ability to empathise with others and the social skills necessary to get along well with friends, family, and coworkers.

People who have reached this level get access to the most recent communication features and methods. Quantum linguistics, retraining, and scientific discovery make up the bulk of their components. It is necessary to have a grasp of individual values, as well as the potential for unconscious behaviour, as well as the reasons for various thought patterns and the strategies used to think them.

Their personality, advanced techniques, and submodalities under advanced NLP are also covered in the course. The mediation abilities as well as any sophisticated language-based negotiating abilities. The scheduled training takes place in many locations and helps to alter relationships, health, and business. And eventually contributes to the growth of a happy existence.

As we went over before, when you pace and lead, you are essentially speaking with the unconscious mind of the person you are working with. It is referred to as unconscious communication since the person you are conversing with is unaware that you are in charge of the tempo and flow of the conversation. This is something that is only conscious to their subconscious mind. In light of the foregoing, it is essential for you to have the awareness that you must under no circumstances put the other person's trust in your communication in jeopardy. When I say that, what I mean is that you must never be so blatant that the person with whom you are conversing detects or becomes aware of the fact that you are matching them or pacing and leading them in the conversation. If someone finds out that you are employing a specific strategy on them, there will be a rupture in the relationship between the two of you, and it is highly likely that this rift will not be able to be patched up.

In passing, I would like to bring to your attention the fact that when I am instructing a course on sales training, I am frequently taken aback by the number of attendees who are seasoned professionals in the field of sales but are unable to differentiate between features, advantages, and benefits. Since this relates to the topic that we are talking about right now, allow me to explain what they are right now. A characteristic that sets one product apart from another but may not be present in other products is known as a feature. A distinguishing characteristic of a product is referred to as a feature. A brown lock with four flaps that interlock might be a good illustration of this concept. The colour of the box, which is brown, is the distinguishing element in this case. The colour of the box can be described as brown because of one of its features. Another feature would be four flaps that interlock with each other. The rationale that behind a consumer's desire for a certain good or service can be referred to as an advantage. For example, the four flaps that interlock with each other prevent the contents of the case from tumbling out. The benefit of possessing this box that has flaps that may interlock with one another is that it will prevent your belongings from tumbling out of the box. The benefit is that you won't have to worry about those things slipping out. A customer makes a purchase for psychological and/or personal reasons, which are referred to as benefits. I might add something along the lines of, "When you store your memorabilia in this box, which has four interlocking flaps, you can be assured that your memorabilia will not fall out, which means that your memories will be safe and secure." This is because the box has interlocking flaps. The benefit that this offers is a safe and secure method of storing meaningful artefacts in a way that allows the individual to feel protected while doing so. The sensations of being guarded, safe, and secure are the emotions that underlie our understanding of why a potential consumer might want to possess that particular box. Understanding the distinctions between characteristics, advantages, and benefits is something that cannot be emphasised enough as being both fundamental and critically vital. People make purchases based on their emotions, and it never ceases to amaze me when I see someone trying to sell something while entirely ignoring the advantages of doing so in the process.

There are schools of thought within the field of hypnosis that assert it is impossible to use hypnosis to coerce someone into doing something that is against their will. In my opinion, this is stated accurately; yet, what is conveniently ignored in this discussion is the reality that hypnosis allows one to bend the will of another person in any way that one chooses. If I am able to sway your will in such a manner that what I offer to you does not go against that will, then it stands to reason that I am able to coerce you into doing whatever it is that I want you to do in some roundabout way. Keeping this in mind, I'd like to go on for a second and talk about different perceptual positions.

This is where feelings start to come into play. At this point, things have the potential to take on an almost mesmerising quality. Have you ever been confronted with a time-sensitive matter that caused you some anxiety, and without even being aware of it, you started having a conversation with yourself in your head about how you felt? It's almost as if you're having a conversation with yourself, but your lips aren't moving. It is a conversation that you have with yourself, and most of the time, you may not even be aware that you are having this conversation with yourself. Sometimes, when I have numerous things that I need to get finished, but I have not yet put them down on paper to serve as a reminder, I find that I find myself carrying on these little mental dialogues with myself, in order to keep me focused on the activities that are currently in front of me. In most cases, I am totally oblivious to the fact that I am engaging in this behaviour. These short conversations with ourselves might actually cause us to become detached from the real world and immersed in our own private little universe. Where we were hypnotised; more specifically, where our consciousness was firmly concentrated in terms of being aligned on what we were doing or thinking about. Thinking about hypnosis in terms of tunnel vision is one of my very favourite ways to approach this topic. When you have tunnel vision, you are essentially mindlessly concentrated in such a way that you are unable to notice anything that is occurring outside of the tunnel you are looking through. When hypnotising a person, a hypnotist will first direct that subject's attention to a single point of concentration in order to start the process. Dr. Milton Erickson's indirect method of hypnosis involved having the subject concentrate on an internal memory, thought, or idea that Erickson provided to them. This was Erickson's method of choice. In early forms of direct hypnosis, the patient would be asked to concentrate on a single item in the room so that the hypnotist could achieve the desired tunnel vision effect. Erickson asserted that the indirect method was significantly more effective after hypnotising a large number of people using both direct and indirect approaches.

Eye Movements Used In NLP For Reading The Other Person

NLP eye accessing cues and lateral eye movements portray a person's internal thought process, which can be easily observed and measured (which is highly valuable in modelling), and may provide insights on how the individual thinks. NLP eye accessing cues and lateral eye movements were developed by Richard Bandler and John Grinder. The individual is sub-communicating when they have the sensory acuity to see the nonverbal cues; it is almost as if they have an X-ray to see through other people's brains!

Knowing about eye accessing cues also helps one to be able to detect dishonesty, which is another application of this information. This programme might not be of much service to you despite the fact that it is not completely reliable. This is especially true if you are dealing with someone who lies habitually or with someone who truly thinks his lies to be true.

The most significant benefit of utilising this technology is the knowledge that it provides regarding an individual's internal processes and the representational systems that they access while communicating. If you are able to determine whether or not a person relies primarily on their visual sense for processing information, you will be able to persuade them more successfully and develop a deeper and more rapid relationship with them.

The Natural Language Processing Accessing Cue Locations

It is vital that you comprehend the fact that the most of people adhere to this particular model. Even if it doesn't happen very often, certain people are organised in a unique way. "People may be disorganised, but they are disorganised in systematic ways," said Richard Bandler, the founder of NLP. Therefore, when you come across these people, simply readjust the custom placements as necessary.

• If you ask a person to remember a memory visually, he will be staring at this 11 o'clock position if you use the abbreviation "Vr" for "visual recall."

- Vc-Visually created: If you ask him to conjure up a visual image that does not already exist in his memory, which means that it must be made up, he will look to his one o'clock.

- If you ask him to recall a sound from his memories, he will glance to his nine o'clock position. This is the audio recall.

- AC – Auditory created – If you ask him to generate sounds, he will look at his three o'clock.

- Ad – Audio digital – Asking him to "self talk" so that he will glance into his 7 o'clock.

- K– Kinesthetic: Getting him to experience a feeling or sensation that you know to be in his 4 o'clock position.

Eye movements that occur laterally in action

Everything you see will take place at breakneck speed while they are processing information within. When you ask a person to feel something (4 o'clock), he will quickly move to possibly visual remembered at 11 o'clock, and then he will briefly ask himself if that's correct 7 o'clock, perhaps his memory is a little dark or blurry (visual sub modality adjustments), so he makes an adjustment by creating artificial lightness so that he goes to the visually constructed position at 1 o'clock.

During the time that he was relating the story about the dog in the distance, his attention was briefly drawn to an adorable puppy. He looked at it and tried to compare it to a dog that he had known when he was a child and had visually remembered.

It is difficult to keep track of everything that is going on since it is happening so quickly; thus, you should practise more in order to become used to paying attention to this degree of data interchange (after all, you are an observer and a communicator at the same time).

related to one's level of competence.

You can experiment with the following mental states by applying them to the spinning disc procedure and seeing what results you obtain.

(a) The feeling that you are free to be yourself and express who you are.

(b) Love – as discussed in the previous section.

(c) A time in which you experienced a feeling of abundance, sometimes known as "abundance," Plenty of friends, plenty of time, plenty of water, plenty of sunshine, plenty of sea, plenty of water, and so on and so forth.

(d) Generous receiving describes a period when you graciously took a gift without feeling obligated to provide something in return. I couldn't be happier to have received the present. Children are naturally skilled in that area.

(e) Expansiveness refers to remembering an experience in which you just felt that you were developing and expanding in either your feelings or your thinking to make room for fresh information or new experiences to enter your life.

(f) Determination refers to the state of being extremely committed to achieving one's goals or finishing a task.

Apply the Powerspin method after assigning a colour to the emotions that were triggered by each encounter.

Consider an instance in which you may have benefited from having more self-assurance as a result of the hue that the Powerspin generated.

Is It Possible That Someone Could Use Our Reality Map Against Us?

After we have defined our world, it is typically much simpler to walk through it and single out all of the characteristics that tend to give each world its own identity. Some people will then begin to take advantage of this kind of individualism in the hopes of attempting to connect with you on a more personal level. They will do this in the hope that they may connect with you on a more personal level. For instance, you might run into a new person who is aware of your fondness for henna tattoos. In an effort to feel more connected to you, this person might decide to get one themselves and show it to you. However, you later find out that they are engaging in this behaviour in order to obtain something from you.

This person is a good illustration of a manipulator. The person who is trying to manipulate you has discovered a way to infiltrate your world by pretending to be someone else that you know and care about. When, in fact, all they are doing is trying to divert their attention so that they can avoid going any closer. There will be times in your life when new people enter it who will cause you to reevaluate the decisions you've made in light of the world around you. They could cause you to wonder whether or not this concept, this new person, or this one-of-a-kind circumstance fits in with your own personal views. Are you certain that you are not going against anything that you believe in when you make this decision? Someone who is more of a master at it will make you question your morality, and then when your beliefs become susceptible, they are going to swoop in and see whether or not they can take advantage of that. If you come across an exceptional manipulator, someone more of a master at it will make you question your morals.

Let's have a look at a real-world illustration of this concept. It's possible that someone you know will try to influence you by turning your faith against you if they are aware that you are a religious person to some extent and they know this about you. They might be able to turn that information to their advantage and exploit your vulnerabilities as a result. They may be aware that violating one's moral code can end up inflicting a great deal of suffering for a person of a certain religious belief. They are even able to make use of guilt and other forms of manipulation in relation to the things that are important to you in order to guarantee that they receive what it is that they desire.

The First Method Is Called Anchoring.

Anchoring is a very helpful NLP method that may be used to induce a specific mental state or feeling in a person. You are free to enter a state of enjoyment, relaxation, concentration, or any other mental state you wish with the help of this tool. In order to successfully implement this strategy, you will typically need to "anchor" it with a touch, gesture, or vocal indication. This anchor functions like a bookmark, allowing you to call up a specific feeling or state of mind whenever you choose to do so at your own discretion.

Let's look at an example of anchoring in order to get a better grasp on how the process actually works. Consider a point in your life when you were particularly content, as this is the first step in this process. Make an effort to recall just one of these experiences. It may be when you won a competition that was really important to you, when you became a parent for the first time, or even when you had your very first kiss. It doesn't matter what you believe to be the happiest time in your life; that will do. Now, give some thought to the times that came before that moment. What were the events leading up to the joyful moment? You should think about the events that led up to that particular moment, make a mental image of it, and try to remember everything you were feeling at that time. Make an effort to be as vivid as you possibly can.

When you reach the peak of these emotions, take the index and middle finger from your left hand and place them in the palm of your right hand. After that, give each of the fingers two light but brief squeezes. When you squeeze them for the second time, try to visualise the wonderful moment in a broader frame, as if it were closer to you than it was the first time. This will help you feel more connected to the experience. Imagine that the sensation is intensifying and becoming more widespread across your body.

After this, all that remains is a game of constant repetition. Make another attempt to explain the sensation, this time focusing on the details of what you experienced at that very instant. The next step is to repeat step one with your right hand, squeezing the same two fingers, but this time increasing the size of the picture. You will find that after some time of doing this, the happy sensation will naturally increase by a factor of two, without your having to do anything to make it expand more. If you are able to conjure up a highly precise mental image of the sensation and recall the exact details of the occasion, you will make much more rapid headway with this technique. If you carry out this procedure at least five times, you will quickly begin to experience the benefits of it.

You have now established a firm foundation. When you have mastered this method, it will be quite simple for you to bring to mind this anchor at any time by just pinching your fingers together twice. Simply thinking about the anchor will bring an immediate smile to your face.

Different kinds of NLP Anchors

There are three distinct varieties of anchors, which are as follows:

1. Visual Anchors In order to elicit a response from someone, visual anchors include exploiting the items that person sees. For instance, if you want to feel powerful, you could use your wristwatch as an anchor. This way, whenever you want to feel powerful, all you have to do is look at the wristwatch and use it as an anchor. However, the anchor does not have to be an object; instead, it could be a person, a symbol, a drawing, or anything else that is physically present.

2. Auditory Anchors The use of sounds or music as anchors to elicit a response is what is referred to as an auditory anchor.

3. Kinesthetic Anchors: One way to use a kinesthetic anchor is to touch yourself or imagine that someone else is touching you.

How to Establish Your Own Personal Anchors

In order to place anchors:

1. Determine the state you want to anchor (the response you want to elicit, such as calmness, happiness, feeling powerful, feeling relaxed, etc.). This is the first step in the anchoring process. It is helpful to put down your aim in your diary so that you can crystallise exactly the feeling or emotion that you intend to generate a trigger for. This will allow you to more effectively achieve your goal.

2. Select the anchor you wish to use to activate that state from the drop-down menu. You are able to employ multiple types of anchors, such as visual and aural anchors, in combination.

3. Bring your eyes to a close.

4. In order to access your resource state, think back to a time when you previously experienced the state that you are aiming to recreate in the present.

5. As soon as you are able to vividly recollect that experience, activate the anchor. You can do this by playing the music, touching the portions of your body that you want to use as anchors, or looking at the object that you want to utilise.

6. Let go of the moorings as soon as you feel the impact of the event beginning to dissipate. It is essential to let go of the anchor as soon as the memory of the experience starts to fade. If you do not, you will end up anchoring a drop in the memory of the experience rather than the experience itself.

7. Give yourself a break and distract yourself with anything else, like counting from one to 10.

8. Perform the steps from step 1 again, but this time focus on making the memory as clear as possible before attempting to place the anchor at the most significant part of the experience.

9. Conduct a test on the anchor to determine whether or not the mandatory condition is met. After you

have refined your process to a point where it is stable, it is imperative that you document every step of the process to ensure that it can be replicated. During this procedure, what feelings rose to the surface? Which of these exact memories have you brought back? You may have used either visual or audible clues, right? Put all you remember in writing.

When seen in conjunction with one another, the experiments conducted by Milgram and Zimbardo provide the following principles, which are the core tenets of boring brain research: people may be easily led, and practises can be influenced in a variety of different ways. This recognition is too distressing for a great many individuals, which is why they choose not to believe it, despite the evidence that proves that it is genuine. The small group of people who are going to take advantage of these ideas are therefore going to go to extraordinary lengths to find a way to exploit the naive masses for their own personal gain.

The concept of 'preparing', which is central to dim brain research, is still another important idea. In preparing, it is said that people might be influenced into behaving with a certain purpose in mind by a variety of factors that are outside of their judgement. For instance, the choice of language that is used when addressing a person has been shown to influence the rate at which they walk a short while afterwards. This was discovered via a series of experiments.

In addition, using words that are pronounced similarly to other words may be an effective way to influence someone's subconcious mental processes without the target being aware that they are being influenced in this manner. Hypnotists like Derren Brown use this method as one of the tools in their arsenal to convince individuals to act in ways for which they have no rational explanation.

In addition, dark brain science capitalises on the human tendency to be defenceless in the face of a more comprehensive evaluation. At any rate, this is the case when the effect in question is present.

against their own sense of objectivity and understanding. against themselves. This was shown by a series of studies carried out by the researcher Asch, who noted that participants' perspectives changed as they were exposed to a larger group of people and how they felt about the topic. This concept of bigger part effect is commonly used by groups that have obsessive belief systems in order to programme individuals whom they desire to influence. When a person is surrounded by other people who sustain particular viewpoints and evaluations, they end up really adopting what they have heard, while at the same time feeling as if they have done so on their own free will. This happens whenever the person is in an environment where such perspectives and evaluations are being upheld.

Administration of Time

When it comes to being able to effectively manage their time, there are two distinct sorts of individuals, according to NLP. Some individuals are able to live "in-time" and are able to enjoy the present without concern about timetables or other forms of time management. Some people spend their lives "through time" and meticulously schedule every minute of every day. In spite of the fact that none of these personality types is inherently superior at time management, persons who are in-time often need to modify their relationship with time. They need to implement more effective time management strategies immediately.

It is necessary for you to adjust your internal conversation if you are an in-timer. expressing things like "It's two o'clock so I should do this, but..." is not as effective as expressing "It's two o'clock so I will do this...." Adopt the mentality of "I will" and focus on dealing with difficulties as they come up. Make use of your innate skill for being present in the here and now in order to tackle things in the here and now. Avoid putting things off or wasting time in any way.

Utilising a planner or calendar to organise one's daily activities is one of the keys to effective time management. Develop the practise of recording significant dates and times in a planner on a regular basis. Then, make it a routine to check your planner first thing in the morning and often throughout the day in order to ensure that you complete tasks at the appropriate times.

You must also acquire the skill of avoiding distractions. Distractions have the potential to send you on a wild goose chase that takes you away from your objectives as well as the work that you are meant to be doing at the moment. Facebook, television, and the many game applications available for download on mobile devices all qualify as significant time wasters. Conceive of these things as annoying time wasters, and construct a barrier to keep them out of your life. Maintain your single-mindedness and concentration on the work at hand at all times.

What Exactly Is The Milton Model When It Comes To NLP And Hypnosis?

The Meta Model, which we looked at in a previous chapter, may be thought of as an inversion of the Milton Model. Its objective is to make the mind more receptive to various other possibilities. And the primary method by which it does this is by being ambiguous in a crafty manner!

The late Milton Erickson

Richard Bandler and John Grinder, the founders of neuro-linguistic programming (NLP), studied and modelled the language patterns of Milton Erickson, a successful psychiatrist and therapist.

The manner that Erickson naturally spoke with his patients was inherently mesmerising. In order to assist his patients in making adjustments, he used ambiguous language and focused on whatever was going on in the room at the time.

Hypotheses and Assumptions

And, the concept that you should incorporate presuppositions into everything that you say is at the core of the Milton Model for language. This is done in the hopes that the patient will start to think the change has taken place as a result of what you have said.

You are getting a better grasp of what I am communicating with you now as you pay attention to my words and listen to my voice.

You learned absolutely nothing from that very final statement. However, it did assume that you were listening to what was being said. And not only that, but the fact that you were listening allowed you to comprehend what was being said.

It's possible that it made you feel all warm and fuzzy inside because to the understanding it provided.

I have no intention of attempting to instruct you in Ericksonian hypnosis, nor even in the proper use of the Milton Model. I just want to provide you with a general overview of the sorts of linguistic patterns that are used by practitioners.

One Illustration of the Ericksonian Method of Hypnosis

Imagine that I am the one saying these things, and then I will explain what I just said: "I know that you are wondering what the Milton Model is. Let me explain."

And it is healthy for you to have such questions.

Because this indicates that you are gaining knowledge in a wide variety of areas.

You are, right?

And everything else that you can learn will provide you with fresh perspectives and new ways of comprehending the world.

Even if you do not believe that you grasp the information, your unconscious mind is processing it and interpreting it. This is true even if you are not aware that your conscious mind is doing so.

The act of deconstructing

Now that we have everything in front of us, let's walk over it and see what I was doing...

'I am aware that you are interested in learning more about the Milton Model.

That was a mind read, which consists of pretending to know what you are thinking while subtly nudging you to really think it.

And it is healthy for you to have such questions.

Who is to say? This makes a claim as though it were common knowledge or something. Often referred to as a Lost performative.

Because this indicates that you are gaining knowledge in a wide variety of areas.

Because suggests a cause and effect that has not been demonstrated, but you may very well come to believe that it does.

And on top of that, I'm going to assume that you are picking up a lot of new information, which means that once again, it coaxes you into believing that it is true.

You are, right?

You have options available to you with only a basic tag inquiry. It gives you the impression that you are in charge, which in turn lessens your resistance.

And everything else that you can learn will provide you with fresh perspectives and new ways of comprehending the world.

The phrase "all the things" is a vast generalisation that gives the impression of something very significant.

A method is transformed into a product through the use of the phrases "insight" and "understanding." It seems as if you automatically get them without having to make any effort in that direction. It's quite simple.

Even if you do not believe that you grasp the information, your unconscious mind is processing it and interpreting it. This is true even if you are not aware that your conscious mind is doing so.

And I found myself in a double bind in the end. This is a statement in which I am successful, regardless of which of two competing possibilities is correct.

You either comprehend what I stated on some level, in which case excellent!

Or maybe you didn't, but even so, your subconscious was able to comprehend it. Very nice!

Visual Methods And Strategies

The visual method is the first one covered in the NLP curriculum. In the next part, I want you to think back to when you were in elementary school and try to conjure up as many as six or seven distinct images in your brain at the same time. Now, invite your buddy to stand in front of you, and when he or she has done so, gaze at that person for ten to fifteen seconds. This endeavour calls for the participation of three individuals: the performer, who is the subject of attention, an absorber, who will observe the performance, and an evaluator. In this particular scenario, I shall play the role of the evaluator. I will inquire with Person A as to whether they would want to stand or sit in front of Person B. The first person, Person A, will make a gesture, and then the second person, Person B, will watch Person A for a few seconds, shut his or her eyes for a few seconds, and then ask Person A to do a new motion. The evaluator will now inquire to Person B about the various gestures that Person A has made and get an explanation from them. In order to complete this exercise, Person A will need to vary the gestures many times, and Person B will need to observe, absorb, and react. The person doing the evaluating will assess whether or not the observation made by Person B is maybe accurate. Person B's observation abilities in NLP terms are recorded after a few repetitions (maybe five), and the sensory and reaction activation can then be analysed. After this, the evaluation is complete. When someone does this exercise more often, they will improve their performance over time. Person B, for instance, keeps track of the route that is shaded by the trees throughout our only run-through of this activity. If we train ourselves to activate our visual reaction, we will see some subtle differences over time.

Rule no. 7: The assumption is that the behaviour you are now engaging in is the best option.

Every modification is made with the purpose of improving things in some manner. You will always choose the option that is most suitable for your present circumstance, taking into account not just who you are but also the things you've been through in your life and any alternatives that you may be aware of. If you were presented with a superior choice, you would choose it if you could, unless doing so would have more severe repercussions or would be detrimental to the environment. If you want to be able to modify a certain undesirable behaviour, you need to have other, better choices available to you, ones that offer a greater number of positives and less drawbacks. The objective is to increase the number of available choices rather than reduce them.

Rule no. 8: Need and want in their proper context

The choices in behaviour that you make should help you become more adaptable and inventive in the pursuit of your objectives, and this should be a goal that they strive towards. You have a propensity to focus more on the things that you desire as opposed to the things that you need. When you do this, you will notice that it is possible for you to be dissatisfied when you discover that what you obtain is not really what you need in the first place. It's possible that you don't get how someone can be great, affluent, and powerful yet still feel like they have no purpose in life. What ends up happening, however, is that these characteristics may have been what the person desired but did not need, or the adverse effects end up outweighing the positive experience.

On the other hand, you may be perplexed as to how some other individuals may still be happy and satisfied despite the fact that they do not own significant riches, power, or outstanding accomplishment. The response is the same. The way in which they choose to interpret the events that occur in their lives allows them to maintain a level of enjoyment despite the monotony of their everyday lives. There is a significant gap between an individual who chooses to think that they are living a straightforward life and another one who chooses to feel that they are living a difficult life. It doesn't matter whether you were born into poverty or not; what matters most is how you dealt with it throughout your formative years.

Rule number nine: Having the ability to adapt to new circumstances

The majority of the time, everyone has access to all that is necessary for them to modify their behaviours. The challenging component is both producing these materials and making them available in the appropriate setting. In application, this signifies that you actually do not need to spend a lot of time and effort trying to get an elite insight into your problems or finding new resources to handle your problems. In other words, this frees you up from having to deal with your problems. The vast majority of the time, you won't have any trouble getting your hands on these materials. The only issue is that they are discussed in very different settings. It's possible that certain activities, like skydiving, which are terrifying and risky, appeal to you more and make you feel more at ease, yet you struggle to feel at ease when you're in social circumstances, which are typically safe and don't pose any risk. You can see that each situation is unique, yet they all have one thing in common: the resources that are accessible. You need merely to access these resources and make use of them in your current circumstance, in which you are not making progress towards getting what you desire. You could, for instance, be able to get rid of stage fright by talking about certain situations in which you feel comfortable and competent. One way to think about this is as transferring your resources to a new setting in which they are required.

The tenth rule is as follows. The act of making something possible.

You have the ability to do a task (behaviour) like speaking in front of a large audience if it is possible for someone else to accomplish it. This is the essence of what modelling entails. NLP was developed in order to help people figure out how they might attain their goals more effectively.

Rule 11 is in effect. The importance of deeds cannot be overstated.

Try to focus more on how the other person is speaking and what they are doing when they are speaking rather than what they are saying while you are conversing with them rather than what they are saying. Listening to the other party's remarks may help you uncover some evidence that is connected to their behaviour. For instance, when you mention that you are interested in going back to your ex-partner, you can have a grimace on your face. So, tell me, what exactly are you thinking? It is far more difficult to fool other people with your actions than with your words alone. When you observe that there is a discrepancy between what the other person is saying and his or her behaviour, this is an indication that there is something wrong. This is a sign that there is something wrong when you notice that there is a contradiction.

Commitment and consistency are the third fundamental principle.

The headline for this concept already contains a lot of information. Consider the following question: Would you want to collaborate with someone who is completely uncommitted to the job that they do? Would you want to collaborate with someone who is so disoriented that they can't produce any kind of coherent work? I'm willing to wager that you would not want to collaborate with someone who isn't devoted to their task or reliable in their performance. This in and of itself demonstrates how vital it is for us to be devoted and consistent with our job in order for us to be able to convince the other person by demonstrating to them how committed and consistent we have been in the past.

Your level of dedication and consistency in the workplace should be the first thing you focus on improving. If you haven't been working on this up until now, then you should give it some consideration and get your act together to make it simpler for you to persuade others; only then will people start trusting your work and like you for it.

The additional advantage of this is that when you continue to be consistent and devoted with your job, it gets recognised in your subconscious mind, and you naturally make it your habit. This is a perk that comes with the territory. Because to this routine, you are able to do your task with ease, comfort, and to the highest possible standard.

When it comes to the application of this concept in the art of persuasion, you need to understand how to get people to agree with you on little matters and get them to answer "yes" to specific questions. The power of your persuasion begins to take effect on them when they begin to agree with you on a number of less significant points. The next step is to convince them to agree to more significant matters and decisions gradually. You have the ability to guide the other person in the path that you would want them to go if you take the initiative. Always keep in mind and make it a point to begin with the smaller fish, and only later go on to the larger ones.

Many individuals will find it relatively simple to put this idea into practise; but, if you find that you are having difficulty doing so, just keep practising until you have it down pat!

Advice To Help Improve One's Communication Skills

It should come as no surprise that you will need to convey a powerful message if you want to influence others and persuade them to listen to what you have to say. If your communication skills are lacking and your body language is not appropriate, you will not be able to accomplish this goal. The purpose of this chapter is to provide you with some pointers that will help you improve not only your ability to communicate but also your body language.

The Words

The first thing to work upon is your language and the manner you communicate. The other person should comprehend what it is that you are attempting to communicate, since clarity is of the biggest importance. Imagine if you are the most powerful person in the room, but no one understands a word that you say. What would happen? They will end up smiling and nodding their heads in agreement, even though they won't understand a word you said. Therefore, you need to work on your language, your ability to give speeches, your intonation, the pitch that should be utilised when speaking, and other aspects of your speaking. Making sure that everything is in order will go a long way towards assisting you in developing a productive channel of communication. If you are unable to enhance your speech, one option that you have is to consult with a speech specialist, who will instruct you on how to talk in a fluent manner. You might also think about attending courses in the same subject matter that are offered online.

Sound Waves

It is essential to possess a strong speaking voice. When you speak, everyone's focus should shift to you, and they should begin paying attention to what you have to say from the very first word you utter. It should come as no surprise that the vast majority of people will be drawn to a baritone. However, you do not need to strain your vocal chords in order to get a low voice. It is sufficient if you are able to communicate properly and draw people's attention to what you are saying.

Walk

I have no doubt that you are familiar with the concept of a Power Walk. It refers to a person who walks with self-assurance. The way you walk alone might sometimes be all that is required to garner respect from others and get their attention. It is imperative that you have a straight back and make every effort to avoid stooping or hunching over. Never glance down at your feet while you're walking, don't put your hands in your pockets, and make an effort to avoid fidgeting with your hands. Take a look around the room at all of the different individuals there. If you look down, it will give the impression that you lack confidence, which is the last thing you want your audience to believe. You can get a better look from a distance to determine whether or not the route in front of you is clear, and then you can start walking. Maintain a straight path while taking steps that are well measured out.

Having A Blank Canvas In Front Of You

When we begin working on a job, it is beneficial for us to have a workspace that is free of clutter. It may be as easy as clearing a table or shutting down all of the windows on your computer before beginning a new project. You are able to do the same thing for your brain. The most fundamental level of neuro-linguistic programming may provide your mind with a clean slate and a new working surface.

The Neuro-Linguistic Programming (NLP) approach is an easy and efficient way to help you cleanse your thoughts. This can be done in a couple of minutes and is applicable to practically every circumstance that may arise in real life.

No matter what it is that you're aiming to do, visualising your success might give you a head start. This foundational NLP concept will serve as the foundation upon which all other NLP procedures are constructed. The power to form mental images of things and bring them to life through one's own creative efforts is what we mean when we talk about visualisation.

Visualisation is a technique that might assist you in gaining mental clarity. It really is as simple as it sounds. The Neuro-Linguistic Programming (NLP) approach is one that utilises your brain to modify your behaviour as well as your internal monologue. Put your eyes out and give yourself some time to reflect on what you've been thinking. If your thoughts are all over the place, it may be tough for you to focus on one thing. Think of anything that motivates you to get things done. Imagine a file box or bookshelf next to a table that is cluttered with objects (representing your ideas).

Now, arrange your ideas in a logical order in your head. Imagine that you are clearing the table of its contents and putting them away either in the cupboard or on the shelf.

It's possible that you're more savvy with technology. Imagine if the tabs on a computer represent your various ideas. Imagine after that you have closed all of those tabs and organised everything into folders. You may picture yourself in a circumstance in which you have to organise and store ideas that are either too exciting or too overpowering. Because NLP is a self-practice, as we said earlier, it enables you to see something that is relevant to you and that you can use as a source of inspiration for yourself.

After you have visualised a clean workstation, either at your desk or on your computer, you may snap a photograph of it. Now think about how much better you feel once you've organised your environment. Attempt to seize the feeling. Now, I want you to close your eyes and picture it. Simply allowing your brain to relax, organise its ideas, and experience a sense of decluttering can help you achieve a level of concentration that will amaze you.

Many congratulations to you! Many congratulations to you! You have just finished the first exercise of your NLP training. The ability to visualise is one that must be honed through repeated practise. On the other hand, the more you practise, the simpler it will become.

When we begin working on a job, it is beneficial for us to have a workspace that is free of clutter. It may be as easy as clearing a table or shutting down all of the windows on your computer before beginning a new project. You are able to do the same thing for your brain. The most fundamental level of neuro-linguistic programming may provide your mind with a clean slate and a new working surface.

The Neuro-Linguistic Programming (NLP) approach is an easy and efficient way to help you cleanse your thoughts. This can be done in a couple of minutes and is applicable to practically every circumstance that may arise in real life.

No matter what it is that you're aiming to do, visualising your success might give you a head start. This foundational NLP concept will serve as the foundation upon which all other NLP procedures are constructed. The power to form mental images of things and bring them to life through one's own creative efforts is what we mean when we talk about visualisation.

Visualisation is a technique that might assist you in gaining mental clarity. It really is as simple as it sounds. The Neuro-Linguistic Programming (NLP) approach is one that utilises your brain to modify your behaviour as well as your internal monologue. Put your eyes out and give yourself some time to reflect on what you've been thinking. If your thoughts are all over the place, it may be tough for you to focus on one thing. Think of anything that motivates you to get things done. Imagine a file box or bookshelf next to a table that is cluttered with objects (representing your ideas). Now, arrange your ideas in a logical order in your head. Imagine that you are clearing the table of its contents and putting them away either in the cupboard or on the shelf.

It's possible that you're more adept with technology. Imagine if the tabs on a computer represent your various ideas. Imagine after that you have closed all of those tabs and organised everything into folders. You may picture yourself in a circumstance in which you have to organise and store ideas that are either too exciting or too overpowering. Because NLP is a self-practice, as we said earlier, it enables you to see something that is relevant to you and that you can use as a source of inspiration for yourself.

After you have visualised a clean workstation, either at your desk or on your computer, you may snap a photograph of it. Now think about how much better you feel once you've organised your environment. Attempt to seize the feeling. Now, I want you to close your eyes and picture it. Simply allowing your brain to relax, organise its ideas, and experience a sense of decluttering can help you achieve a level of concentration that will amaze you.

Many congratulations to you! Many congratulations to you! You have just finished the first exercise of your NLP training. The ability to visualise is one that must be honed through repeated practise. On the other hand, the more you practise, the simpler it will become.

A sly one Person Who Is Deceitful

The bad guys are the bad ones. Problematic are dishonest people who engage in manipulative behaviour. Take, for instance:

A mean girl makes an attempt to bring down the social standing of a decent classmate.

She tells the other students in the class that the individual was engaging in some heinous behaviour.

A friendlier fellow student is less popular.

The sympathetic fellow student is sad.

Example 2: Playing Tricks with a Happy Attitude

The use of manipulation may make everyone in a situation seem more attractive.

Tricksters with experience are known as party people.

Someone who is having a good time bumps into someone else.

A person at the party laughs disarmingly and apologises to the other person, even though the other person was in the wrong.

The party person avoids fighting and enjoys a wonderful evening as a result.

It's not her manipulative behaviour, her malevolent aim, or the falsehoods she spreads that are the problem with the case of the cruel girl.

Please hear me out on this: Have good intentions.

My presumption is that you will use the strategies with honourable goals in mind. I ask that you kindly comply.

Body Language and Mental Attitude

The human brain is a judging organ, and it uses this ability to evaluate information. Throughout the course of evolution, this has been the factor that has allowed humanity to survive. We form an opinion about that person in a split second: Is he dangerous?

Is the guy appealing to look at?

Is that specific person a socially necessary user for my continued existence?

Be wary of this impulse, but under no circumstances should you act on it until you have a solid grasp of the individual. The manipulations that are about to be detailed will cause you to behave in a way that is admired by others.

This section does not mainly focus on body language, but the patterns discussed here have a subconscious impact on how people present themselves physically.

Every individual has the right to be respected, until it can be shown differently.

Again, if you treat other people with respect, you have nothing to lose and everything to gain by doing so. That does not imply that you are expected to spend the whole day fondling boots; rather, it suggests that you shouldn't dismiss someone or make them feel like they don't matter.

Just like everyone else, up to the point when they no longer merit it.

The benefit of the doubt should always be given to outsiders. In our reality, there is no need for someone to physically resemble the role that they play. I came in contact with some nice-appearing jerks and millionaires, all of whom behaved like excited children. Examine the book's cover, but make sure you read at least a few pages before passing judgement.

Neither the scumbag nor the millionaire can be said to be "better" than the other. But being around one of them made me feel depressed, while being around the other made me feel happy and energised.

Manipulation Of Emotional States

Feelings and emotions are fundamental to the fact that we are human beings. In spite of the fact that the majority of us make an effort to present an image that is robust and menacing in this cutthroat world, we are nevertheless susceptible to a variety of emotions. We are all guilty of doing it. And yet, many individuals admit that their emotional moods play a larger role in their decision-making than their ability to rationalise their choices using cold, hard reasoning. People who are skilled at emotionally manipulating others take advantage of this predisposition by using a wide variety of methods, tactics, and procedures.

The most effective methods of emotional manipulation are covert; this means that they are constructed in such a manner that they influence your behaviour, character, and attitudes without you being aware of it. It is a sneaky strategy that works so profoundly that it many times penetrates your awareness and burrows so deep that it reaches your subconscious. It is a way that operates so deeply that it operates so deeply. Do not let yourself be misled by people who are attractive and pleasant in your presence just because the sight of their grin causes your determination to dissolve into a puddle everytime they talk to you. Your relationships with them may appear as natural as your contacts with any other person, but you should be on high alert. They might be your employer, a colleague, a friend, or even a cousin.

You'll come to understand that even actions that don't seem to be harmful might have extremely adverse effects. For example, you may have a buddy with whom you find it difficult to discuss unfavourable emotions that you are experiencing or anxieties that are keeping you up at night. This may be the case. This may be the case since this buddy constantly reflects a conscious optimism on everyone else around him, and perhaps even frowns when you express anything bad around her as if you are tainting her aura or depressing the spirit of everyone else. It's possible that your first instinct is to consider this quality to be beneficial or favourable. This buddy is attempting to get you to stop focusing on everything except the positive aspects of your life because, as you probably already know, life is too short to waste time griping about the negative aspects of your life, many of which are beyond your control.

On the other hand, if you give this situation careful consideration, you'll see that there is a great deal of manipulation going on behind the scenes. Because of this buddy, it is difficult for you to speak your mind and convey the things that you actually feel, simply because they may not register well with this person. This friend makes it tough for you to speak your mind. They want to maintain their mental and emotional equilibrium at all costs, and as a result, they will do whatever it takes to isolate you in your own headspace so that they may do it in a way that makes them feel good about themselves. It is hard to believe, but this person's constant smile and upbeat attitude may just be a defence mechanism. This is an example of manipulation.

There are some individuals who may manipulate others on occasion only for the sake of gaining some immediate advantage or usefulness, while other people will manipulate others in an unhealthy and pathological manner. Even when they engage in pathological manipulation on a consistent basis, some people may be unaware that this describes their behaviour. In the viewpoint of these individuals, other people will never amount to anything more than tools, hence there is no chance that they will ever experience love or closeness with another person. People who are narcissistic, psychopathic, and Machiavellian are said to be members of the "dark triad" of psychology. This term was coined by psychologists. These people are heartless and uncompromising, harsh and insensitive, and they are ruthless. These 'dark triad' individuals are detrimental to the mental balance of everyone around them because not only do they bend other people to their will in overt and covert ways just for their personal gain, but they may even go so far as to ensnare you with a charming personality even as they brainwash you into submission. This is because they are only interested in themselves and their own personal gain.

You will be exposed not only to the methods that emotionally manipulative people use, but also to practical insights on how to deduce emotional manipulation if, for example, you are currently a victim of this. This is true regardless of the category of manipulators that you may come across or interact with in the course of your daily activities.

Recognising When You're Being Manipulated Emotionally

Every kind of manipulation depends on the same underlying tactic, which is to coerce you into doing in a way that you normally wouldn't. You are a unique individual with your own set of values, preferences, tendencies, and limitations. It is the job of an emotional manipulator to con you out of these fundamental characteristics of who you are, to the point that it becomes very difficult, if not downright illogical, for you to make choices that are congruent with these fundamental components of who you are. Your personal autonomy has been violated, and you are no longer able to make choices that are in your own best interests after giving them serious thought.

You are dealing with an active manipulator if you have a supervisor who constantly challenges your IQ or a colleague who makes sarcastic remarks about your work wardrobe. Doubt is a fundamental tool that is used by those who engage in emotional manipulation. They prompt you to begin calling your own perspective and decisions into question. They destroy your feeling of self-worth and self-confidence to the point where you lose respect for yourself and stop respecting the aspects that make you unique. They do this by suffocating your sense of self-worth and by damaging your self-confidence. In extreme circumstances, these individuals make you so insecure and yet pose themselves as the rescuer and fixer of what they created wrong with you, so that you go out of your way to seek their adoration, playing yourself into their hands in the process.

Basically, emotional manipulators use your own emotions to bring you down from the inside. They stir up love, trust, admiration, fear, shame, and guilt. They stir up these strong emotions and use these to chip away at your sense of personal identity until there's basically nothing left of the original you. And all the while they conceal their malicious intentions, while going the extra mile to decipher your vulnerabilities and then using this vulnerabilities to make you into a pawn in their hands.

Hence, you must take care to pay attention to those times when you begin to doubt or questions your instincts and perceptions. You must try to deconstruct those moments of vulnerability to determine the forces accelerating the emotional explosions going on inside of you.

The psychological term for adept emotional manipulators is "puppet masters." They are so deceptive and subtle, yet they have such talent at playing your emotions that they can mislead you into doing things while giving the impression that you are behaving freely. The majority of people who are misled spend years feeling in their hearts that something is off, but they are unable to pinpoint the specific cause. You can protect yourself against emotional manipulators now that you have a glimmer of what goes through their brains.

Manipulation In The Course Of Our Everyday Lives

- The underhanded strategy of manipulation is something that we are confronted with on a daily basis. People who manipulate others want nothing more than to have their wants satisfied, but they are willing to resort to dishonest means to achieve this goal.

- Those who were manipulated as children or who grew up in an environment where manipulation was common find it difficult to understand what is really going on. This is because, if you are experiencing manipulation again, it may seem familiar to you. It's possible that you were manipulated in a prior relationship, or that the relationship you're in right now is triggering memories of your upbringing for you.

- It is essential to understand this since manipulative strategies induce breakdowns in communication and erode a person's confidence in others. Instead of being straightforward about what's going on, people will often look for opportunities to manipulate the situation and engage in petty games. On the other hand, some people place a high value on communication for the sole purpose of using it as a tool to manipulate the circumstances and draw attention to the other person's shortcomings so that they may maintain control. This is something that often comes up in discussion among persons of this sort. They are not interested in hearing what others have to say about themselves, and they are not there to provide assistance to the individuals who are struggling with whatever it is that they are dealing with. In this particular scenario, establishing one's supremacy is the only thing that matters.

- The following is a selection of strategies that may be used on a daily basis:

- The following is a list of some of the more typical types of approaches that we may encounter:

- Lying includes telling white lies, untruths, partial or half-facts, exaggerations, and truths that have been stretched out of their original context.

- Love Flooding is the act of showering someone with praises, love, or attention in an excessive manner. This is also referred to as "buttering someone up."

- Love denial is conveying the message to another person that they do not love you while also withholding your own love and affection from them until you achieve your goals.

- Removing oneself from the situation, either by completely ignoring the other person or by isolating oneself from them and being mute.

- Providing individuals with several alternatives in the hopes that it would divert their attention away from the one choice that you would like they not select is an example of choice restriction.

- The practice of trying to persuade a person to behave in a way that is completely counter to what you want them to do in the hopes of inspiring them to act in a manner that is completely counter to what you wanted them to do in the first place is an example of reverse psychology.

- Being condescendingly sarcastic or having a patronizing tone is something that, to be honest, all of us are guilty of doing from time to time. However, people that are influencing others in dialogues will do this on a continuous basis. They are making fun of you, and their tone makes it seem like you are a kid. Additionally, the things that they say to you are demeaning to you.

- Speaking in Generalizations or Universal Statements - The manipulator will take the remark and make it wrong by dramatically expanding it in scope. People and objects that are included in a group are eligible to be the subject of generalizations. One might feel more connected to a general remark.

- A universal example would be something like, "You always say things like that." A generalization would be something like, "Therapists always behave like that."

- Luring and then Playing Innocent - Either we or someone we know is skilled at manipulating the emotions of the people we care about the most. On the other hand, a manipulator will try to manipulate their partner by pushing their buttons and then will pretend as if they have no clue what occurred. They immediately elicit the response that they were hoping for, and it is at this point that their partner has to pay really careful attention to what it is that they are doing. Those that are abusive will continue to act in this manner again and over until their partner will begin to question whether or not they have lost their minds.

- Bullying is one of the most obvious types of manipulation, and it is also one of the most common. Take, for instance, the scenario in which your partner requests you to clean the kitchen. Even if you don't want to, the look that they give you suggests that you should clean it or face the consequences. You tell them that you'll clean, but the reason you say this is because they just used some type of violence to get you to do what they wanted you to do in the first place. They may have informed you afterwards that you had the option to decline, but you already understood that you were powerless to do so. It is vital to note that if you believe that you cannot say no in your relationship without worrying for your safety, then you need to leave the relationship. If this is the case, you need to end the connection.

Using the Love in Your Heart as a Weapon against You Your partner has discovered a stray kitten and is eager to welcome it into the house. The next obvious step would be to explore whether or not you would be able to provide housing and money for the cat. However, they choose to approach things in a deceptive manner. Their end objective is to make you feel guilty about not being able to care for the animal properly. Do not allow anybody, not even your husband, convince you that you are unable to make the decision that is in your best interest. If you don't want to, you don't have to feed or clean up after the kitten at all. In a nutshell, you should respond to their tactics with rational alternatives.

"If you love me, you would do this for me," the message said. This one is particularly difficult because it puts to the test how you feel about your partner in marriage. They are trying to manipulate you into feeling guilty and ashamed by asking you to demonstrate your love for them by giving them what they want from you. In this predicament, the only thing you can do is completely cease doing it. You don't need to go out to the shop in order to let your partner know how much you care about them. They could have easily asked you to leave if that was what they want.

Emotional Blackmail is an unpleasant and harmful kind of manipulation. The concept that someone you care about can hurt themselves if you abandon them is, at its foundation, dangerous. They want to maintain their control over you, therefore they are playing on your feelings of guilt, fear, and humiliation. Keep in mind that you are not solely responsible for ensuring the health and happiness of anybody else. You have to keep reminding yourself to not be fooled by it. This is a manipulative strategy that will never change. On the other hand, you may inform them that in the event that they get the sense that they are going to hurt themselves in any way, you would call an ambulance to assist them.

When it's Convenient to be Needy – Has your partner begun to feel sick or upset when they don't get what they want? This is a straightforward method of psychological manipulation. For example, they don't want to go anywhere with you, and then all of a sudden they have a panic attack that you have to assist them get through so that they don't get to go anywhere at all. This is not at all healthy, and if it continues, you should strongly consider quitting the relationship as soon as possible.

They Don't Let Difficult Circumstances Get Them Down - Whenever someone is harmed or when someone passes away, your spouse never seems to respond with any kind of emotion. They never lose their composure. When someone is subjected to this kind of manipulation, they begin to question whether or not their responses are appropriate, or whether or not their feelings are within their control. Because no one else should be allowed to tell you how you ought to feel, this is a controlling mechanism. This may give the impression that they are calling into question your mental health and maturity level, particularly if you find yourself seeking to them for guidance on how to react to certain scenarios. If this is something that happens to you frequently and you notice that you keep falling for it, you might want to consider making an appointment with a therapist. By doing so, they will be able to assist you in working on your emotional reactions and finding your genuine sentiments once again. This sort of manipulation may do significant harm to your mental health. Learn to go with your instincts for the time being. It will not lead you in the wrong direction.

This strategy of manipulation consists of two parts: first, you tell them that everything is a joke. Your partner will say painful things about you, and then when you become angry, they will get irritated because you can't handle a joke and they will continue to say nasty things about you. Sometimes, they will make jokes about you in front of other people, and if you don't react favorably to the jokes, you will once again be the one to spoil everyone's enjoyment. This is a method for repeatedly putting you down without having to accept responsibility for what they are doing. Keep in mind that by speaking out for yourself in this situation, you are not spoiling the enjoyment for anybody else.

Forcing Their Insecurities Upon You – Here, for example, your spouse will deceive you into believing that their insecurities are now your issue and will use them as a method to dominate you. They will do this so that they can maintain their own sense of power and control over you. They will tell you that they have been cheated on in the past, which is why they do not want you to retain male friends and that you should stop doing so. They will also advise you to quit keeping male friends. Or they use them to regulate your behavior when you behave in a specific manner because they don't want to lose you and they don't want to lose you. In light of the circumstances, it is necessary for you to establish a middle ground. You may care about someone and make sure that you are respectful of their emotions, but you should not allow yourself to be misled into feeling what your partner wants you to feel, even if you are in a committed relationship. The feeling of guilt drives all of their deception.

You Are Held Responsible and Accountable for What He or She Feels As a Result of This. – This strategy of psychological manipulation is pretty amusing since your partner spends a lot of time getting you to believe and feel as if you are unable to think about your thoughts or their feelings on your own and that you need to be reminded of how they feel in order for you to do so. They will tell you how they feel about you and that you are to blame for how they feel about themselves. If they are upset, it is because of you that they are upset. You are responsible for how they are feeling; you must have done something to provoke it. They take a lot from you and tell you how you feel, but then they expect you to be accountable for how they feel. This strategy belittles you not just because they demand a lot from you, but also because they tell you how they feel.

It not only makes you want what they want, but it also makes you believe that it is what you want. Relationships need compromise from both parties. On the other hand, it is not typical to have to entirely sacrifice what you want in order to placate your partner and make it possible for you to fully commit to what it is that they desire. If you start to notice that your needs are being satisfied far less often than those of your partner, it's time to start asking some questions about the situation. You need to ask yourself whether you are giving them what they want because you want to or because they made you feel guilty or a feeling of culpability for how they feel. whether the answer is the former, then you need to question yourself why you are giving them what they want in the latter case. If you realize that you are willing to sacrifice everything for them, then you need to reevaluate what it is that you regard to be most essential in your life.

Historically Notable Instances Of Deceit

One of the most widespread applications of dark psychology is deception as a technique. We find examples of deceit being utilized throughout practically the whole of human history. The strength of deception and deceit is well shown by the story of the Trojan horse. A entire populace was under the impression that they were going to get a present, but instead they were killed in a massacre.

The growth and collapse of Elizabeth Holmes and her health technology company Theranos is one of the most prominent examples of major events that have emerged as a result of a dishonest foundation in the contemporary era. Holmes said that he had developed a blood testing device that could do comprehensive diagnostics using just a trace quantity of blood, most often obtained from a fingerstick. Even though these people weren't random people off the street, Holmes managed to mislead all of her investors and board of directors totally.

As potential investors in Holmes's biotech company, billionaire media tycoon Rupert Murdoch, the Walton family of Wal-Mart fame, and the Davos family, pioneers of Amway, all fell for Holmes's deceptions and lost their money. She was even able to deceive several wealthy and well-educated members of the board, including numerous previous or future members of the Cabinet of the United States Presidential Cabinet. When it was proven that Holmes' miracle blood testing technology was fundamentally faulty and may have even put the health of the individuals who had depended on it at danger, the house of cards that

Holmes had built came crashing down around her. Before the truth about her falsehoods came to light, Holmes had amassed a net worth of $4.5 billion, which she has now lost entirely.

Somehow, Holmes was able to fool some of the most well-known businesspeople and scientists in the United States as well as the rest of the globe. That is some real dishonesty right there!

I want you to go back over the course of your life and recall three different moments or incidents. The first one should be a period when you felt like you were at the peak of your physical and mental health. This is the point of the exercise at when your breathing, movement, and energy levels should be at their highest. When you think back to that period of time, make an effort to relive it by experiencing it via your senses of sight, hearing, and touch. Think back to another period in your life when you were incredibly pleased, and do it while you are clinging to this sensation of being in perfect health. This may have been a moment when you were with key people in your life, or it could have been a significant event that gave you a lot of happiness. Again, you should make the most of your ability to see, hear, and feel it via your eyes, ears, and body. Keep this notion in mind at all times. Now remember back to another moment when you accomplished a significant goal that marked a turning point in your life and you felt a sense of accomplishment and empowerment. This may be anything as basic as cleaning the garage or kitchen, or it could be something more significant like graduating from school or a program, or completing some exciting journey. Again, try to remember this in as much detail and with as many associations as you can. Imagine that you have commissioned someone to compose a theme song or tune for you as you continue to bask in the sensations of wonderful health, unbridled joy, and a sense of success. Continue to do this while you continue to focus on these emotions. This might be something incredibly creative, or it could be a song or piece of music from the past that was one of your favorites. Permit that song to play in your head as you revisit that period when you were at the peak of your physical and mental health and had accomplished everything you set out to do. Imagine that you are taking in the vibrations of the music, and that you are experiencing and seeing any colors that are linked with being in such a great mood. You can maintain that condition for as long as you wish if you want to.

Consider why you are in this condition while you take in my words and think about how the exercise brought it about. Consider the implications. Intellectually comprehend the concept. Consider the fact that you have produced a resource, which you will now want to evaluate. And to put it to the test, choose an occurrence that you believe will take place in the foreseeable future. It's possible that you recognize that this is the moment when you're going to be put to the test. It might be a period in which you are aware that you need to perform to the best of your abilities. Or it might be a period when you are aware that you must exhibit strength in order to get through it. When you think about that period of time, let your mind start playing the tune it remembers. This is the music that you have permanently linked to the moments in your life when you reached the pinnacle of health, happiness, and personal achievement. Take note of the ways in which your sentiments start to shift. Take note of how much control you have and how capable you are of making better decisions in life.

Methods For Influencing The Mind

Having control over everyday situations is something all human beings wish for. The ability to command what will happen is the dream of most people. Although it is impossible to accomplish 100% of the time, some techniques allow you to achieve the desired results more often. If you did not already know, it is possible to influence the activities of another person via the use of straightforward behaviors and signals that are sent directly to the target of your influence. You may put these pointers to use in conversations with your manager, during job interviews, or even with that friend you have a crush on!

1. Honest Smile

Do you know how to offer a flawless grin, despite the fact that you should already be aware that smiling is one of the most essential and vital components of body language? Some smiles are visibly forceful and hostile, so you should seek to convey the truth. But how can we maximize this action? Simply said, you should maintain your regular visage and, after just a few seconds, welcome the guy and offer him an authentic grin. Whoever grins the most has the potential to obtain more emotional control over the other person, who will also feel more at ease in his company if he does so.

2. Look

Do not be afraid to draw your attention to the person of your interest while you are among a group of friends and that person is there. Do not hesitate to do so. When you focus your eyes on the other person, you will automatically catch their attention eventually. If you know how to gauge your looks, it will soon be within your power to get their attention. Keep your gaze fixed on the eyes of the person with whom you are conversing, whether you are at a job interview or speaking with the employer. Doing so will raise the likelihood of the other person experiencing more empathy for you as well as higher trust in you!

3. Refuse to give up.

Your ability to convince your friends will astound you, and you will be amazed by this ability. Have we not previously discussed the well-known proverb that asserts, "A lie that is told a thousand times will eventually be believed?" However, despite the fact that we are not dealing with falsehoods, you are able to adapt this statement to the approach at hand. If you want someone to take what you say seriously and trust what you say, all you have to do is emphasize their perspective. Take for instance the scenario in which you want to offer a goods but first need to demonstrate why customers might consider doing so. If you want to convince your customer of anything, there is no use in being persistent and bringing up the same points over and over again since doing so will make you inconvenient. Instead, focus on expanding the number of compelling reasons why you should be believed by adding more strong points to the argument.

The fundamental nature of who we are.

The component of plants that grow on soil from which you may get nutrients is called a root. Our identity may be compared to a plant that has its origins in neurolinguistic programming, which is also the source of the nutrients it needs to stay alive. These are things that begin with our views, such as "this is to give credit to an event or as safe and secure news," and they often feed on philosophies, religions, and political ideologies. Here we can deduce that what a person believes is where fully places trust which itself is and will be a reality, know each takes the data necessary and beneficial to himself and builds its own area, indicating that event, event or news becomes your reality, for example, petit were told that if we played in the street when it rained we could get sick, then every time it rains and gets wet in the rain, in the belief that we are going to get sick is activated.

"Those who persecute will always be able to seize the opportunity when it presents itself."

H. Jackson Brown was his name.

A set of beliefs

Edgar Allan Poe once said that "We only know what is the consolation of heart, but when we are alone."

1- Convictions

We can see, as a living example of the beliefs held by every human being, how these beliefs are organised in the various cultures and religions that are practised around the world, in both the East and the West. Everyone places their utmost faith and confidence in either one item or one person. Religions have constructed a collection of human laws that impact staff inside each person. These regulations include the manner in which people should dress, the foods that should be consumed at festivals, ceremonies, and the punishment for women who commit adultery, amongst other things. They are intended to maintain human life and the development of each individual within social groups: some restrict personal growth and human development, others limit equality, many pieces of Justice, but regardless, everyone chooses to construct his own world using the resources that are available to them or as they see appropriate for themselves.

In terms of private ideas (such as "who am I? Who am I? What are the bounds of my existence? What is my truth?), you cannot necessarily religiously specify how a collection of ideas are joined to believe in anything like our own thoughts, shortcomings or strengths, or maybe someone: a loved one, a god. With these beliefs, we unconsciously reaffirm our belief in who and what we are, as well as what we want to be and what we want to accomplish; we also see how many hierarchical our ideas of what should be our way of socially organised are.

Then, when all of this is said and done, it is that the nutrients we receive through our five senses and processes of our brains begin to bear fruit. This fruit is projected in our speech, perceive, and think, and this is where it starts to break down the complexity of our minds and give rescheduled based on the resources of our judgement NLP.

In this way, we can observe that man evolves and changes in accordance with the beliefs that he has. Your beliefs will reach a specific degree based on the level of their psychological and social growth. People tend to see their beliefs as their own reality, something to the credit of the truth in what is confirmed or denied; for example, via our beliefs, we might be assured that we know we have the power to take care to do anything, including accomplishing our objectives and desires. We are able to construct our personal, societal, and cultural identities with their help.

4. Develop a sense of awareness and ask yourself, "Well, now what?"

After you've stopped struggling against life, you could take things a step further and say, "Alright, this is happening; what should I do now? "

That one small complication is incredible. It redirects your attention from fighting against what is happening to concentrating on finding a solution to the problem. This is the point in time when something will take place. You are tapping into the power of both your conscious mind and your unconscious mind at the same time. The answers will present themselves to you while you are either playing, resting, or dreaming. In addition, you see that it takes a greater amount of energy to argue than it does to find a solution. Gaining momentum is a constant aspect of forward motion.

In this particular instance, absolutely. Since I was about a decade old, I've had major back problems, including spinal fusion surgery. I never stopped believing that my back will get better on its own eventually. But that wasn't the case. In the end, I came to terms with what was happening, went and had x-rays and other tests to see how severe it was, and when I got the findings back, I made the decision that I was going to heal myself naturally. That was the first step in my journey to become a yoga practitioner. And it completely eliminated my persistent back pain!

5. Acknowledge the fact that there are challenging conditions that you must check

There has to be a change of mindset. Living is not about cruising through life making cheap money via street banking and performing to your heart's delight without any consequences. Things that are going to go wrong are going to be difficult. Illnesses, injuries, deaths, losses, betrayals, divorces, and disappointments are just some of the things that will inevitably befall you at some time in your life. What is more important is not so much what you see as what you do with what you see.

If things become difficult, you need to make the decision to push through them. When things become difficult, keep in mind that you have a choice: you can either choose to struggle or you may choose to progress. Cheer up when things are difficult because they are going to get better for you.

This entry was written in my journal after my second episode of psychosis in a month, which occurred two days after I woke up in the Acute Psych Ward of Lion's Gate Hospital, where I had been committed and was unable to leave on my own.

"There is going to be a ray of sunshine in my life once again, so there!

Defiant, yes, and yes again. However, I was aware that in order to make it through this challenging period, I would need to draw into the energy that is focused and centred inside me. I had no choice but to take a stance, and in order to prove to myself that I was capable of carrying it out, I had to put it in writing. I am in possession of it.

Studies in Neurolinguistics Programming is an organised study of human performance, and by using methods from the field of neuro-linguistic programming (NLP), it is feasible to enhance, change, and remove experiences that are subjective and deceptive. The NLP framework enables you to undergo profound alterations inside your psyche and assists you in maturing into a more admirable individual than you are right now.

In the early 1970s, a young psychology student named Richard Bandler was attending the University of California, Santa Cruz. If you want to study more about the history of NLP, a good place to begin is with Richard Bandler. NLP, or Neuro-Linguistic Programming, is a kind of therapy that was developed by him and Dr. John Grinder, a linguist. They did this by combining the ideas, methods, and procedures of three prominent therapists.

Fritz Perls, Virginia Satir, and Milton Erickson were the three distinguished psychotherapists whom Grinder and Bandler collaborated with throughout their careers. Richard and Bandler were fascinated by the ideas and methods of three different therapists, so they did a lot of research on their work and the outcomes they achieved. Let's take a look at these three different people one at a time before we circle back around to Bandler and Grinder.

Fritz Perls was a Jewish psychotherapist and psychiatrist. Together with his wife Laura, he established the Gestalt Theory, which is one of the primary ideas that underpins NLP. Laura Perls was also a psychotherapist and psychiatrist. The following is a list of some of the characteristics of NLP that may be traced back to the impact of the Gestalt Theory:

The importance of nonverbal communication Spatial sorting, which refers to the physical space between people and how this influences actions The importance of asking the 'how' question rather than the 'why' question, how is an individual doing what he or she is doing instead of why

The following thought-provoking quotations can assist you in gaining a deeper comprehension of Gestalt theory:

1. Anxiety is just excitement that is not accompanied with oxygen.

2. Neither we nor anybody else is here to meet the expectations that others have of us, nor are they here to meet the expectations that we have of them.

3. When we are dependent on other people, particularly if that dependence is

for the sake of boosting our self-esteem, we give up our freedom and become slaves. If we seek the acclaim of other people, then that implies that each and every one of them gets to be a judge.

Virginia Satir was a social worker, an author, and a family therapist who held the belief that the world might be fixed by mending families. Satir was also a proponent of the idea that families are the foundation of society. When Richard Bandler was working on editing and transcribing the transcripts of Fritz Perls's writings, he had the opportunity to meet an incredible lady. Because he was so taken with her ideas and the way she taught, he decided to videotape a whole workshop that she was leading and then utilise some of the strategies that he learned from that workshop to replicate the strategies that are used in Neuro-Linguistic Programming. The following is a list of some of Virginia

Satir's concepts that have been incorporated into NLP:

Family therapy has the potential to repair the world, but the concerns that are brought up in sessions are seldom the primary source of the difficulty. The way in which a person is attempting to deal with a problem is more likely to be the source of a problem than the problem itself.

A person's personal power is determined by the congruence of all of their internal parts, including their emotions, words, and behaviours. For a change to be meaningful, it is necessary for the individual as a whole to be involved in the process. A lack of self-esteem may be a significant factor in relational and behavioural problems. Satir classifies people according to the prominent personality traits that they exhibit, and the categories include the following:

Blamer – the authoritarian who is also pointing fingers Placater – one who will do all that it takes to keep the peace Distracter – one who can't focus and is constantly changing subjects and cannot sit still Computer – also known as the super reasonable, this person is completely disconnected, just like a computer Distracter – one who can't concentrate and is constantly changing subjects and cannot sit still Computer – also known as the super reasonable

Equaliser - a person who maintains a level head in all circumstances and concentrates on meeting the demands of the here and now

You may connect more with Virginia Satir's views and concepts of psychology by reading some of the intriguing quotations that she has written. Here are some of such quotes:

1. We all need at least four hugs a day in order to stay alive, eight hugs a day in order to stay the same, and twelve hugs a day in order to improve ourselves and develop.

2. The way life really is is not at all what one would expect it to be. Simply said, life is as it is. The way in which you deal with it determines the outcome.

3. Do not let the narrow perspectives of others determine who you are.

In addition to being a hypnotherapist, psychologist, and psychiatrist, Milton Erickson was also a practitioner of hypnotherapy. In addition to that, he was the first person ever elected to the presidency of the illustrious American Society of Clinical Hypnotherapists. The following are many of Milton Erickson's concepts that have been included into NLP:

It is not feasible to tell others how they should feel; all you can do is point them in a specific direction. It is crucial to communicate as precisely as possible, leaving as little space for ambiguity as possible. Using the problem itself to discover its answer gives you the best results. Using the problem itself to find its solution offers you the best results.

Richard Bandler and John Grinder - These two incorporated the approaches from the aforementioned three persons, as well as those from Alfred Korzybski and Gregory Bateson, in order to develop an NLP Meta model. This model was given in two volumes and included the following components: Richard Bandler and John Grinder.

1. A Book About Language and Therapy, Structure of Magic, Volume I

2. A Book About Communication and Alteration, entitled The Structure of Magic II

Bandler and Grinder articulated their idea that therapy sessions done by these prominent therapists and linguists had a structure that could be taught to people in suitable models to enhance the quality of their lives in these books. They believed that this structure could be taught to individuals to help them improve the quality of their lives. NLP training has the power to correct distortions, eliminate oversimplifications, and bring more clarity to one's knowledge of the human mind. As a result, our lives and the connections we have with one another may become much more satisfying.

What was started by Bandler and Grinder in the 1970s has today become a pervasive way of life. Additionally, more and more techniques are being developed by specialists in the field, and an increasing number of people are reaching out to leverage the power of NLP and putting it to use in both their personal and professional lives. Training individuals to become NLP coaches and practitioners is one of the primary focuses of the hundreds of organisations that can be found all over the globe.

NLP And Education

Neuro-Linguistic Programming (NLP) and other similar applications may be used effectively to improve the educational outcomes for students, teachers, administrators, and the network as a whole. Blackerby (2002a) acknowledges that we have presupposed that students understand how to learn in the study hall and carry out the academic assignments we give them, but often they don't, and a large number of students have been injured as a result of their inability to succeed in school. Art (2001) acknowledges that NLP provides a constructive and logical view on learning as a way for becoming consciously more viable on the planet, and that this perspective may be used by students of any age. We are able to make use of social adaptability by using NLP standards, which allows us to proceed towards the instructional process in novel and stimulating methods.

The States of Learning

According to Dryden and Vos (1999), learning develops swiftly and efficiently via pleasure and curiosity in an environment that promotes learning through the variety, shock, creative mind, and challenge. This environment fosters learning through the all-out environment. Numerous experts and educators agree that the alpha brainwave state, which consists of 8 to 12 cycles per second, is optimal for reviving long-term memory by beginning the process of subliminal learning (Dryden and Vos, 1999; James 1996). This is the range that is considered to be the most effective for this purpose (Dryden and Vos, 1999;

James 1996). Researchers have shown that complex music may activate alpha, mostly due to the fact that the basic 60 to 70 beats per minute of this music are comparable to alpha (Bandler, 1986; Stockwell, 1992). GeorgiLozanov, a therapist and educator from Bulgaria, built a significant portion of our continuing knowledge about using music to encourage states into a learning position that he dubbed suggestopedia (Luzanov, 1978). In an investigation conducted with the United States Armed Forces, it was shown that Suggestopedia was unsuccessful in teaching German at a rate of 661 percent, achieving more than twice the results in less than a third of the time as standard German language instruction (Dryden and Vos, 1999).

The similarities between NLP and Lozanov'ssuggestopedia, as well as Rita and Kenneth Dunn's instructional framework that adapts to a person's learning styles, have been compared and contrasted by Dunn and Waggoner (1995). According to Dunn and Waggoner (1995), these approaches are united in their belief that the manner in which academic failure is caused by the way in which institutions instruct their student body. All of these approaches acknowledge that one's mental state may influence their ability to learn and aim towards cultivating optimal learning environments for their students.

Educational Applications of Neuro-Linguistic Programming (NLP)

According to Dilts and Epstein (1995), the overarching goal of applying NLP to education is to provide a core framework that is aligned with the observable experience of learning and prepared settings in order to increase the efficacy and speed with which objective situated learning may take place. By focusing on effective correspondence with strategies for developing one's own perspectives on topics (Craft, 2001), NLP establishes connections between ideas, thoughts, and behaviours and their respective goals and aims. Training, from the perspective of NLP, is seen as the interaction between the critical processes by which we achieve individual health and greatness, as well as the acquisition of new skills. This incorporates using aptitudes for the purpose of producing aware and oblivious talents by means of the foundation of new initiatives and approaches (James, 1996). This encompasses a wide variety of topics, from difficulties in learning and other concerns to exceptional learning programmes and accelerated learning. It is essential to cultivate skills that build on the how and why of finding out how to begin developing such talents as early on in life as is practically possible given that the content of learning is always shifting, and it is crucial to do so because it is essential to keep up with the changing nature of the learning itself. According to Dilts and Epstein (1995), the application of NLP to educational settings ensures coverage in the following areas:

The fundamental requirements for education

Processes of a fundamental neurosemantic nature that are involved in learning

Forms of dynamic assessment as well as self-evaluation

Different tiers of education and methods of education

Learning via interaction and other types of beneficial learning

Different aptitudes and instructional approaches are shown here. Instruments for education and other educational devices

Applications of NLP in education provide fundamental tools and systems that may assist persons in updating, acquiring, channelling, and retaining new facts in a manner that is consistent with and advances through time (James, 1996). According to Dilts and Epstein (1995), the core applications of NLP to educational settings revolve on the principles of dynamic learning. Understanding is essential to dynamic learning, which is why the two go hand in hand. According to Dilts and Epstein (1995), the process of dynamic learning include learning by doing, researching different tactics for speculating, and acknowledging that the relationships that exist between persons are an essential component of the learning process. Dynamic learning tools highlight the abilities of cooperative learning, co-training, and tutoring, which is essential given that learning occurs via doing. If you have a desire to see, then demonstration is the way to go. According to James (1996), dynamic learning approaches are those that make use of the presenting criteria and tools of NLP. These strategies are designed to release natural learning skills by way of attention, exploration, and revelation. It is emphasised that the presentation of decision as being vital to activity is a key aim and that the expansion of decision is a significant objective (Craft, 2001). According to Dilts and Epstein (1995), the following outcomes are associated with the use of NLP to educational settings:

recognising and developing one's own unique characteristics

Improving one's ability to remember and think creatively

Creating the optimal conditions for learning and instructional methods

Taking into account safeguards against education

Developing beliefs that facilitate learning and growth

Determine which beliefs are limiting and try to recast them. associated with educational pursuits

The administration of mediations for staggered learning.

Changing things that were disappointing into something that were great feedback

investigating different kinds of intuitive learning

Coercion has a tendency to modify behaviour, but mind control (Coercion persuasion) affects the attitudes, beliefs, thinking processes, and behaviours (modify of personality). This is the primary reason why mind control is more successful than other forms of control. Highlight: The victim willingly and actively helps to assist and participates in the process of change because they believe it to be the most effective course of action. As time goes on, it becomes more difficult for them to accept the possibility that a person in whom they had placed their faith may have been dishonest with them. Because of this trust, mind control may occur without being seen by anybody. Even when the manipulator is no longer present, the victim will still maintain the learnt ideas, attitudes, behaviours, and personality traits since he or she feels that the choice was made totally by him or her. The effects of choices that we have taken ourselves have a longer lasting influence than those that we are well aware were pushed for by another else. In addition, it is not easy to acknowledge the fact that the choices you consider yourself to have taken were, in reality, heavily impacted by the actions of another person. Even more so if it was a buddy who played a prank on you.

The majority of people who manipulate others via the use of mind control methods will reassure their victims that they are not being coerced or threatened in any way. As a consequence of this, the victim is led to feel that he or she made the choice of their own free will. The belief that neither party is coercing the other into doing anything is a very strong one, and a manipulator will constantly hunt for opportunities to take advantage of beliefs like this. Anyone who isn't familiar with the tactics of mind control won't have a leg to stand on when arguing that they were subjected to manipulation. The individual who is being deceived will have the perception that they are free to make their own choices and that no one is imposing these choices on them. We are thrust farther into the false world that was produced by mind control, and this is due to the fact that the choices that we have made for ourselves have more power than those that have been made for us by others.

Although it is possible that you will not be the target of a manipulator, you are likely to be subjected to a range of typical manipulation methods on a regular basis. Every one of us is vulnerable to some unethical types of manipulation, and these may take many forms. Some forms of manipulation that we experience on a daily basis include the following:

Having the person who is victimising us provide us with a number of options, all of which ultimately lead to the same result. For instance, a salesman could provide you with a few different bundles, but the end goal is always the same: the acquisition of a product.

It's possible that the person trying to manipulate you will keep using the same phrase over and over again in the hopes of implanting it in your mind. The longer someone listens to something, the more refined and understandable it will become to them. The goal of the manipulator is to get you in a state of comfort so that they may subsequently control you. When an idea takes root in your head, the person trying to manipulate you will exploit that to their advantage.

A manipulator may use emotional manipulation to put the victim in a heightened state of emotions to the point where he or she cannot utilise reasoning while making decisions. This can be accomplished via the use of emotional blackmail. The manipulator of brainwashing exploits the victim's wrath and terror to gain control over the victim. However, in order to manipulate someone's thoughts, the manipulator will exploit feelings such as love and despair. For instance, a manipulator might make their victim feel horrible or worthless if they do not cooperate or do what the manipulator deems to be the "right" thing.

The manipulator has the ability to make you feel as if the world is about to come crashing down on you at any moment. He or she demonstrates to you that the only way out of the predicament is to follow their suggestions. In his advertising, he often features innocent-looking youngsters, and he also employs certain types of music and voice tones for the purpose of selling.

As you went through these strategies, you could have recognised one of them as one that has been used over and again in the context of your area. A political party or a new company may have a slogan that they often repeat in a way that makes it easy to identify with the phrase the first time you hear it. A news station is able to convey information by repeatedly broadcasting the same message. The majority of marketing organisations are not using tactics of manipulation in order to transform you into a mindless robot; nonetheless, they are increasingly affecting the majority of our judgements.

These deceptive practises may be found in every sphere of human activity. If you are proactive, though, you won't have to worry about falling victim to these forms of manipulation and control. This is the good news. First and foremost, avoiding tactics of dark psychology requires staying away from the manipulators themselves, which may be challenging. How are people supposed to escape commercials when they are literally everywhere? It may come at a high financial cost to skip the commercials yet continue to watch TV. In light of this, the most effective tactic you can use is to steer clear of the things you can and to work on striking a healthy equilibrium with the rest.

"What Was It About The Other Presenters That Didn't Impress You?"

As the participants enter that negative frame of mind and give me their responses, I tilt my body slightly to the left and pretend to shove that sensation off to the right side with my hands. It's more like avoiding the unpleasant sensation altogether. Repeating the same gesture each time I am given a negative response is a habit of mine.

Have you taken note of the way in which I've grounded the good and negative sentiments in various ways? Because I opted to point towards myself when I made the motion, the pleasant sensations that were there were rooted in me. On the other hand, when it came to unfavourable emotions, my default reaction was to avoid them and push them away. The catch is that now whenever I have a casual discussion with them, I may activate any happy or negative sentiments in them at any moment by utilising these two triggers that I had created. This applies to both positive and negative feelings. This occurs as a direct result of these stimuli having now been recognised in the subconscious mind. I had used these hand signals several times during the session, and since their attention was focused on me, their subconscious minds had been conditioned to respond to them automatically. When your subconscious mind observes me doing these motions again, it will instantly stimulate that specific sensation in you that was previously connected with that gesture.

You may be asking how exactly this relates to marketing and sales in any way, shape, or form. You may set the triggers during your client meetings in exactly the same manner that I did during the seminars and get the same results. When asked about their experiences with a certain product, consumers and clients will provide either a favourable or negative response. If they are speaking in a positive manner, you should establish an anchor that is pointing towards you. Then, if they say anything nice, you should utilise that motion. You may employ the opposite sort of motion, which is like you are pushing away the bad energy away from you, if the customer is not pleased with the goods and the business and are complaining about it. That is what I did during the course of the session, and you are free to do the same if you so want. You will be able to trigger the pleasant sensations and correlate them with your product and your organisation after these gestures have been ingrained in the subconscious mind of your customer.

If you have your items in front of you throughout the meetings, another intelligent gesture that you can do is to lightly tap on the product each time anything nice is spoken. You may utilise this gesture if you have your products in front of you. This tapping will serve as your trigger in the future.

When working with customers, this is one of the easiest methods to get them to associate with you and establish a favourable anchor towards you.

The third task requires you to take a seat somewhere quiet and think about how you may use this strategy in real life. Put in writing the several contexts in which you may use this strategy, as well as the steps you would take to implement it.

The concentration of a single idea or thought is what hypnosis is.

Our brain/mind can only consciously think about one thing at a time. After then, the surrounding world, other people, and noises in the background, among other things, become "invisible" to us. When you concentrate on what you want to do, your attention will become frenzied at various points, to the point where you will be completely unaware of everything else — unless, of course, you have a pressing need for it to shift to other things. That is the most profound level of hypnosis you can achieve! It does not stray from the central notion or concept at any point. This is a level of total absorption and concentration. The term "selective thinking" is used to describe this state of mind rather often. When a person is in a state of selective thinking, everything that is not directly relevant to the present thought processor and does not constitute a danger to the individual's safety or ability to survive is filtered out of awareness.

What I Mean by "Full Focus"

This is precisely what it means to be in a state of total focus. You are only aware of one thing, and the only thing that is occurring in your mind at any one time. Every other stimulus will be disregarded or disregarded entirely. Concentrating on what is on TV and scarcely knowing the dialogue outside is hypnosis. Neither watching television nor listening to what other people are saying someplace qualifies as hypnosis. When you're so engrossed in a book that you don't even notice when someone else walks into the room, you're in a hypnotic state and it doesn't matter whether they try to speak to you. It is not possible to achieve hypnosis by conversing with someone while thinking about what other people are saying. When you are listening to someone's voice, you are not in the least bit distracted by other discussions, the passing of traffic outside, or the ringing of a phone in another room... It has a hypnotic effect. People are aware of other stimuli throughout all stages of hypnosis, even though there is no concentration on them other than the stimuli that are required for the state. This is why everything seems perfectly normal during hypnosis. Even in the most profound hypnotic state, it is possible to have this form of consciousness, which is characterised by an acute awareness of an absence of any kind of concern or interest. After that, you will finally be able to start recognising your hypnotic condition.

Manifestations of Hypnosis That Can Be Seen

The majority of people are curious about what it is like to be hypnotised, however the reality is that there is no sensation associated with being hypnotised. In addition, there are no blinking lights or other indicators to let you know when you have entered the hypnotic state. It's not like you wake up one day and think, "Yes, I can tell you." That is not how hypnosis works at all. Nevertheless, you can find yourself experiencing the following emotions:

A state of complete and total relaxation across the whole of the body.

I couldn't tell whether I should have felt heavy or a bit weightless.

The rate of breathing often slows down, becoming more consistent, and shallower.

It's possible that more than one person may sense a tingling feeling in their fingertips.

The passage of time appears to be sped up or slowed down, depending on how you look at it.

Increase emotional arousal, suggestion, and realization.

Your own conscious or subconscious barriers might determine the extent of the altered state of consciousness you experience during hypnosis. since of this, it is sometimes argued that "all hypnosis is self-hypnosis" since hypnotists can only direct you to the degree that you allow them to. The encouraging news is that you do not need to enter a profound state of hypnosis in order to get the benefits of our self-hypnosis recordings. You will induce a hypnotic state in yourself by focusing, particularly if you are willing to face the possibility that you will not feel hypnotic.

How to Make Your Dreams Come True Using NLP Techniques is the Topic of Chapter 10.

Since the debut of the movie "The Secret," the concept of the Law of Attraction has taken over the business that deals with self-improvement. Before then, there were not even a fraction of the number of gurus that there are now who are advocating for the relevance of the Law of Attraction. As a consequence of this, some of our NLP practitioners are cautious to combine their recently learned NLP tactics and processes with the principles of the Law of Attraction.

Are the principles of NLP and the Law of Attraction incompatible with one another?

Not! On the other hand, NLP is a useful addition to the Law of Attraction.

It is necessary to have a clear mental picture of your objectives before you can go on with the process of turning them into a reality.

In addition, learning NLP will teach you a visualisation method that will dramatically improve your ability to see things more clearly in your mind's eye. This is a method from the field of neuro-linguistic programming (NLP) that illustrates how mental rehearsal works.

NLP Visualisation Technique with 5 Steps to Follow.

1) Determine your target. Know exactly what it is you want. First things first, you need to have a clear idea of what it is that you want to achieve. If there is a reason why so many individuals fail to achieve success in life or when adopting NLP approaches, it is because they are unable to recognise their own motivations or aspirations.

2) You have to be able to see, hear, and feel oneself carrying out the job or accomplishing the intended objective exactly how you want it to be done. Imagine yourself at first as a mental picture that is separate from yourself. This suggests that you need to be able to identify yourself in the picture that's been provided. When you are in a condition of dissociation, it is probable that your feelings are less obvious.

3) By practising with each of the many submodalities, you may make the overall experience more intense. When discussing neuro-linguistic

programming (NLP), the term "submodalities" refers to the more nuanced differences that may be made in how one communicates utilising their five senses. You might theoretically produce a variety of submodalities, including the following:

* The size of the picture in pixels.

* The location at where the photograph was taken.

* When you felt confident, were there any particular things that you were visualising?

* Different aspects of the image's lighting, etc.

Your first aim should be to bring out as much brightness and intensity in the picture or video as you possibly can.

When used with increased degrees of specificity, the visualisation approach used in NLP will prove to be more successful.

For instance, try increasing the size of the picture as well as the brightness of it to get the desired outcome.

Does it make the wonderful experience you have had even better? What do you think about moving the picture in a little bit closer to where you are? Does it make your conclusion more compelling to listen to or to follow?

www.ingramcontent.com/pod-product-compliance
Lightning Source LLC
Chambersburg PA
CBHW052139110526
44591CB00012B/1785